AND STILL THE SKY IS PINK AND BLUE

AND STILL THE SKY IS PINK AND BLUE

BY JOAN HILL

AND STILL THE SKY IS PINK AND BLUE

Published by Joan Hill, Edmonton, Canada

ISBN:P
Paperback 978-1-77354-540-0
ebook 978-1-77354-541-7

Publication assistance by
PAGEMASTER PUBLISHING
PageMaster.ca

Contents

SECTION 1
Blackbird Soar Outside My Window....1

Searching....2
Children....3
Visitation....4
Shadows....5
Labyrinth....6
Knife Edge....7
Grandfather....8
Relocation....9
Windows....10
One Of Those Bright Days....11
Risen....12
Flutter....13
Dark Thread....14
Presence....15

SECTION 2
Prairie Roots....17

Prairie Roots....18
Black Hollow....20
Stalked....21
Father....22
Rattling....23
Fragile People....24
Uncle Stanley....25

SECTION 3
First Home....27

First Home....28
Echoes....29
Thanks For The Tea....31
Back To The Land....32
And Still The Sky Is
Pink And Blue....34
From The Window....35

SECTION 4
Uneasy Rhythm....37

Sleek Pearl....38
Adrift....40
Demons....41
Let Go At Fifty....42
A Kind Of A Touch....43
Uneasy Rhythm....45
Casualties Of War....46

SECTION 5
Woman In A Wedge....47

Woman In A Wedge....48
In Shades Of
Black White And Grey....49
The Streets Of This House....50
This House Once
Meant So Much....51
This Is The Year I Grew Old....52

SECTION 6
Remembrances....53

Idle Things....54
Coast Range....55
His Last Year....56

Introduction

The poems in this manuscript reach back to my prairie roots growing up on a farm in rural Manitoba and begins with the story of my grandmother, tracing the thread of mental illness that unwittingly shaped our family life.

Due to growing up with my mother's struggle to come to terms with her mother being sent away to a mental home, the trauma of losing her husband to suicide and her own eventual battle with mental illness, I found acceptance of this legacy of illness and its passage through my sisters and I and our children.

The audience for my manuscript is for those who encounter mental illness in families, its far-reaching effect, how to keep loving and the learning of compassion.

Section 1

Blackbird Soar Outside My Window

Searching

Today I'm anxious and tossed
like tumbleweed sweeping
across the open prairie
hoping to uncover
some link, some reason,
some light in the thread of darkness
stitched through my family.

The Niord sailed for the new country
in 1890 with my grandfather on it.
His fare paid by an uncle in Lillehammer.

At eighteen he was young and strong
with umber colored hair
and deep brown eyes.

He met Anna, a young widow.
They settled in the Black Hills
of North Dakota where
the sun set early
and warm light beckoned
in farmhouse windows.

Children

They had six children.
Albert, the oldest, then Clara,
my mother, Mary, Stanley and
two boys named Harry.

The first Harry lived only a few days.
When the remaining Harry died
years later in the same asylum, plagued
by the same illness as Grandmother
the hospital records gave his date of birth
as that of the baby who died.

Maybe that other self
was one of the whispering voices
in his head.

Visitation

Why did you send
your scourge
to devastate my family
when I was only
eight years old?

Voracious
as the swarm of grasshoppers,
the scourge descended
on our farm
covered fields, gutted crops,
left nothing untouched.

After the visitation
I walked through flattened
rows of corn
and scarlet runner beans
most of their leaves gone.

Perforated
with fine holes
forming a pattern
almost like letters.

Shadows

Wind wraps darkness round me.
I race across the heavens with Aavak,
Norse God of the sun, God of the dawn.
We chase my fear of madness toward morning.

The spirit of my grandmother
brushes past me,
where fiords stretch
long narrow fingers
into the land.

Even as a child
shadows had begun
to reach inside her.

Labyrinth

Grandmother's life became a maze
through which she struggled.
The specter of depression always ready
to block out the light.

Sometimes I fear
I walk that same labyrinth
afraid I'll lose
my own sweet stillness.

Knife Edge

I think of her
nursing a new baby
trying to follow God's teachings,
to escape dreams
of the devil.

Looking out of the kitchen window
peeling potatoes for dinner
children fighting outside
Grandmother runs to the door
clutching the peeling knife
wanting to stop the noise.

Children see the knife,
scream that Grandma
is going to kill them.

Grandfather

Grandfather took Grandma to a doctor
who said that she should
be put in an asylum
until she was over these episodes.

Grandfather had her taken away
was told
never to visit
never to allow
the children to visit.

My mother
the only daughter at home
at age 14 took over
the care of the household.

She never
visited her mother
until she was an adult
with a husband and children of her own.

Relocation

It was like putting the sun
in solitary confinement.
The doctor spoke of it
as Grandma's "relocation".

It's a long way out of the city
with the policeman driving,
and the lady from the church
in the back seat beside her.

City lights fade one by one
pavement ends
becomes a bumpy road
with ruts so deep
she hopes
the tires will get stuck
and they will have to call someone
to take her back home.

Windows

The asylum has many windows
lined with black bars.
She climbs the grey stone stairs,
carries a paper sack with
"Essentials"
Sets of two:
Vests, drawers,
brush and comb,
cotton dresses.

Her Sunday dress
ivory-pink with a sage green sash
and lace trimmings
saved for church
and holiday dinners
with the family.

Saved for the day
she will return home
stand once more in her living room
watch the blackbird
spread its wings
soar outside the window.

One Of those Bright Days

For twenty-seven years
behind black bars
Grandma watched
the seasons change—

The violet of spring
with its first new crocus
the buttercup yellow of summer
the gold of autumn
the glistening silver
of sun on snow.

She died in January
on one of those bright days.

Risen

No one in the family
talked about Grandma.
It's as if she never lived,
never held a man close,
never sung lullabies
to her children.

Locked away
Grandma grew pale
sick with waiting
when no one came to visit.

I dreamed this morning
that she had risen
from the ashes of her confusion
on wings clear and white—
wings that brushed my cheek.

Flutter

In the family album there's
a black and white photograph
of my mother at age fourteen.
Thick dark hair spirals down her shoulders
her eyes appear fathoms deep.

The hope of finding
her mother waiting for her
after school with a bright smile,
cookies, a glass of milk,
her dreams of becoming a singer, dashed
the day Grandma returned
to the home
for the last time.

Mother went once,
was allowed to wave
from the grounds below.
All she could see
was a flutter at the window.

Dark Thread

I awoke this morning thinking–
a thread from the past
has woven its way
into my life and that of my children.

My son at four years old
had an imaginary friend
named Anna.

He was too young to know
that his great grandmother
spent twenty-seven years
in an insane asylum.

I made him give up
his Anna.
Now I think
I sent Grandmother away
for a second time.

Presence

Grandma's voice hangs in the air
murmurs through the walls
of my house
and those of my sisters.

We want to deny
that her life was as hollow
as my footsteps in the empty church.

The wide mahogany floorboards creak,
my footsteps echo in the empty church.
The presence of my grandmother is near
her face uplifted to the altar
toward a globe of light
behind a stained-glass window.

I hear a faint chant–
The words of a hymn
"The sacred Christ
whose glory fills the skies
bring thy glory down
The sacred instrument Christ
fill me with radiance divine
scatter all my unbelief
The sacred day
bring it nigh
when thy mercy's beams I see"

Hymn from The Anglican Prayer Book
Source unknown

Section 2

Prairie Roots

Prairie Roots

On mornings like this
the sun spins marsh grasses into gold.
I walk my dog to the bird sanctuary.

She leaps ahead, disappears
into a rippling sea of yellow.
Prairie roots lead me back
to wheat fields honey gold
rows of burning chaff
Mother and me
silhouetted against red sky.

Days when she'd pick
strong shafts of straw
left over from the burning,
teach me to make pipes
from corn husks.

I'm swept back
to my uncle's house on highway 59
somewhere between Winnipeg and Birds Hill

To Uncle Stanley hurling a pitchfork at rats
big as cats, eyes flashing.

Early mornings
30 or 40 degrees below zero
as he cranks the old blue Ford to life
pigs squeal inside

bright marble eyes peer
through swaying slats.

We groan out of the driveway at 5 a.m.
sun just beginning to meet
open fields and drifting snow.

Prairie Roots published in
"Goldsborough Families" - 2010

Black Hollow

As a child I felt afraid
to make too many ripples.
I clung to my corner of the universe.

Did Mother feel as insignificant as I,
as she suffered waves of highs and lows—
broken like that black earth
the chaff plowed under each fall?

She said she could feel
the lows approaching.

On her highs my mother
showed my sisters and I
how to make dolls, copper jewelry,
taught us to sew, paint figurines,
make mosaic plaques.

Then the lows would descend.
She would go to bed for days,
often voluntarily, commit
herself to the psychiatric ward.

I remember seeing her at the window.
She would wave to my sisters and I
then disappear
into the black hollow.

Stalked

On clear nights I could hear the yip, yip
of coyotes, their staccato howls,
often the mewl and cry of a lynx
or one of our cats, then silence—
one of them had been caught.

For weeks there would be
no cries in the night
then all-of-a-sudden
another cat would be gone
the coyotes had struck again.

Sometimes they came close to the house.
One day, just outside the kitchen window
I saw my pup, Brandy, being dragged
up the mountain.
I screamed, the coyote dropped him.
He survived but from that day on
stayed close to home.

I think of my mother's illness
stalking me, my family
waiting outside the door.

Father

In my dreams
my steps echo
as I climb the stairs,
walk along a hallway,
search for the open door.

When I enter
the fireplace is cold
the room empty.

I see the same window
in every dream.

The panes are dark
I search for the man
who jumped
from nine floors up.

Father killed himself
when I was two years old.

Rattling

Sometimes
when the wind
is rattling the windows
and the house is cold
I get up early.

I dig out the old clippings
feel I am there on the 9th floor
in late March
where my father sits
inside—
alone by the window.

He made the front page
though bombs were exploding
in the Rhineland.

One must have
gone off in his head
that day.

The headlines said
"Man Plunges 9 Floors to Instant Death"

Fragile People

Fragile people
made of glass
shimmer in the light.

In my dream
I feel them splinter.

Grandmother
spent days pacing up and down
the lonely halls of an asylum.

Mother, a cut crystal
eclipsed from her mother,
plagued too by depression.
It left her
an echo of herself.

Father
whose bones shattered
plunging from a building.

Uncle Stanley

He was the youngest of a family of five,
watching silently
as his brothers and sisters
wrestled
with their demons.

Uncle Stanley was the one
Mother ran to
when father killed himself.

He was our rock–
spared for some reason.

Maybe there really is a God
who, in this family design
found the compassion
to leave one whole.

Section 3

First Home

First Home

"Not far now
only a few miles
up the Valley"
the real estate man said.
Ahead of us
a winding road
snow, sparkling white in places
grey and dirty in others.

In front of us
a small house
shingles worn, weathered
two dilapidated sheds
a barn with boards turned silver
a chicken coop
gnarled wire fences
rotting posts.

"It's kind of rustic"
the real estate man said.
I looked into your eyes
that spoke of
straight fences
chickens clucking in the yard
green pastures, grazing horses.

I glimpsed painted trim
window boxes overflowing
with bright flowers
lace curtains fluttering in the breeze.

Echoes

Sometimes the sounds return.
A cock crows
it's shrill cry
waking Jess and Candy
whose rasping hee-haws
join the chorus of jays
chattering high and blue
outside the window.

November sun,
a white ball in the early morning haze
enclosed my world–
that kitchen, that farm
surrounded by cedar trees,
mountains dabbed with light,
faint hum of tires on the highway
a mile away.

In that spacious kitchen
I mused over choosing
a solid oak table
at least four feet across,
big enough for all the children
I would have gather round it,
voices rising in high-pitched chatter.

In the hush of morning
I would bend over crib slats
press my face close until

I felt the baby's breath
soft on my cheek.

Tiptoe downstairs wanting
to cap the silence
preserve it
like the pears
lined up in jars on the counter,
gold caps gleaming
in the dimness of the stove light.

thanks for the tea

On the news today
the broadcaster announced,
there's a threat of war in Iran—
reminding me of draft-dodgers
from the Vietnam war
who secrete themselves in log cabins
high up in the mountains of this valley.

My son has a friend named Freedom.
His parents, thankful that their son
will never have to flee his country
never be drafted
into that war in Iran
any war.

Reminding me that our sons
growing up to be men,
will never have to go to war
no matter what the future brings.

Thanks for the tea
I'll come again.
Let's hold on tight
to what we have now,
not talk of war or death,
let's just talk of husbands, children
and growing old.

Back to the Land

Long rides on horseback
roads that wound their way
along mountain paths
the smell of woodsmoke
surprise on finding a log cabin
tucked away in a blaze of cedar trees
juice fresh from the apple press.

Until then I never knew
people still lived in mountain cabins
with no electricity, no running water,
no furnace to turn up at dawn.

I lay awake at night
fearing to hear
pounding hooves, shrieking horses
crashing garbage cans, bears snorting
outside the door.

Couldn't help but rage
for baby pigs born
when the storm came—
their mother
trampling them into the ground.

Couldn't save the young bull
even with nightly vigils
wrapping blankets round him
pouring whiskey down his throat.

The moon was ablaze
the night he died
and if you didn't know
you would have thought
nights there were beautiful.

And Still the Sky Is Pink And Blue

A warm summer day
late afternoon.

A young goat
tied to the laden apple tree
lies white against the red fallen fruit.

Tugs at the rope
frantic, eyes bulge
a dog's worried bark calls.

I arrive too late
cut the tired one loose
rest my head on the still warm body.

And still the sky is pink and blue
bathes the mountains
spreads out like melting icing.

From the Window

You said you knew
all about farming
when we moved to that place
with rotting fences
couch grass and sow thistle
nearly to the roof of the house.

I thought it could be a home
once the grass was cut
weeds pulled
daffodils and tulips planted
a path cut to the meadow.

All I remember is killing
chickens, cows, pigs, dogs.

Like the coyote pup I found
up by the spring
yellow eyes staring
as I placed a bowl of meat
in the clearing, near as I could
without frightening him away.

It took a week to coax him down
though you warned me
he would be after the chickens.

I saw you from the window
big hands reaching for him
under the truck.

Then you grabbed your rifle
your face rigid
as you knelt down
carefully took aim.

Section 4

Uneasy Rhythm

Sleek Pearl

Tonight I'm like a planet
strayed from orbit.

Prowl around the house
in this hour before light.

Here in the city
neighbouring houses
box me in.
I yearn for open space,
colors and shapes of the country.

Outside a bark
fills the room with an echo
of my old dog in the Slocan Valley
500 miles away.

I see her young again
sleek pearl
curled up near the wood stove

Her eyes, bright suns
draw me into that other world
where I rode horseback
in the mountains.

She was a dog who loved to run
would disappear into the pines
that flanked the trail.

Then round a bend I would see her
white against the slate black earth
a bright moon
to direct my path.

Adrift

Evenings like this when the sun is setting
accompanied by a chill wind
that jostles the apple blossoms
from the tree in my backyard
I think of her, my friend in the Eastern Arctic
who follows the trail of dog sleds
from her perch in a Twin Otter
two thousand feet above
a frozen landscape.

She says she is too old to be adrift like this,
midwife to young Arctic women, content
with the natural progression of their lives.
Unlike them, she finds herself alone
in her mid-forties, her husband
a thing of the past, her children
out on their own, her life scattered
like those apple blossoms.

I would like to take her with me, along
that clean dirt road that led us back
to a pink-dyed meadow—
race again those dove grey ponies
the length of the field,
feel our bodies flow
with the horses' easy rhythm
down a clear and certain trail.

Demons

This started out as a simple poem
about a friend searching for
her demons.

I'm trying to write about my friend
but my own demons keep surfacing.

I left my husband a year ago
thought I had dumped
all thoughts of him
in the lake,
threw him overboard
with all his belongings
in an old black suitcase
as frayed and worn as me,
watched him sink to the bottom.

My friend's demons are elusive
like silver trout
that dart between weeds
in green water at the lake.

She wants to dredge them up,
talk to them,
maybe settle the score.

While I hold mine down
under satin smooth water
solid as plate glass
though they scratch and cry
to be freed.

Joan Hill

Let Go At Fifty

My sister tells me
she no longer
looks for a job.

Says she is bothered by ghosts
of children she has counseled,
drives again the winding roads
to outpost schools.

Says she rises from her bed
wanders down the hall
to the kitchen.

Employment agencies,
closed doors, city streets
have etched their shapes
into her face.

She makes herself a cup of tea
sees the days ahead pour out
heedless of her.

A Kind Of A Touch

In the restaurant
after the night crowd has faded
light from the lamp outside
reveals a splendid red sun
blazing over a mountain lake
in the stained-glass window opposite.

It nudges a longing for the Valley
packed away years ago.

I can almost feel the wind
breathing through poplar trees
tall and slender
shooting green-gold leaves
into the sun
see cherry blossoms
like snow on the ground.

Remember how the beauty faded
like the mirage on the highway
where further round that bend
the farm stood
at the end of a twisting road.

There's a hole in the fence
where the cow broke through,
paint peeling from boards
of the chicken coop,
gate hanging by strands of wire

clinging to a post
loose in the eroding earth
flooded by winter's runoff.

How, when winter crept back,
friends were the only warmth
in chilling whiteness.

I can still see my friend
as I reached her cabin,
smell the coffee—
her smile warm as heat waves
emanating from the wood stove.

This stained-glass image unlocks
part of me remembering
those friends whose lives
intertwined so closely with mine—
that the hush of light shining
on the window
is a kind of touch.

Uneasy Rhythm

My daughter turns
seventeen this spring
says she's grown up.

Every Sunday morning
she rides horseback
at the stable
on the outskirts of town.

Tallest girl in the class
poised and sure of herself
glides over each jump.

Her eyes scan
the group of parents–
defy me still.

Years earlier
she looked to me for help
that day we rode to the sand flats
above the farm.

Her horse kept straining at the reins
in a hurry to climb the hill
pulling
as she does now
away from me.

Casualties Of War

We sat across from each other
in the dimly lit restaurant.

My son's expression tight,
his eyes
a blue wall of silence.

My daughter's hostility
a cold draft
that has swept in
from under the door.

As mustard-colored walls
compress us in a booth
I see my children rush back
to the years that had trampled
like a relentless army over
their innocent worlds—

My adolescent children
strike back at their enemy.

Words of defense
rise in my throat.
I clench my teeth
sit in silence
want this war to be over.

Section 5

Woman In A Wedge

Woman In A Wedge

She said she had a dream of me crying
because my hair had been cut too short,
it stuck out in all directions.

I try to find meaning,
but curiously,
my drawings have overtaken my dreams
appear with minds of their own.

A soft over-stuffed sofa
a winding staircase
viewed through shattered glass.

A woman's shape
wedged between
a tall white building
and a house.

In Shades Of Black White And Grey

Somewhere between a city street
and a sun-filled interior
my drawing sweeps
across tall buildings
that sway as if rocked by winds
then settles lightly
on a sunlit threshold.
I am drawn inside.

The Streets Of This House

My body moves through
the dark corridors
of this house.

This house
holds the cookie jar my daughter gave me
in the shape of a cat
with transparent blue eyes
who sits cold and still
on my kitchen table.

The picture of my son
at age sixteen.
He stands defiant, rigid,
looks at me with reproachful eyes.

This house encloses—
drawings
this woman,
caught between narrow aisles
where walls converge,
and walking is dangerous.

This House Once Meant So Much

If I would now stand
outside this house
and draw a picture.

Inside there would be
shapes of doors
placed at odd angles to the floor
colliding with images of
pictures that hang askew
on my living room walls.

There would be no kitchen chairs
just dark lines
reduced to sticks
upon which
no one would sit.

The windows
would be black spaces.

This Is the Year I Grew Old

This is the year I grew old
knocked down by those
who claimed
they meant no harm.

Though when it came to saving me
each took his bite
trustee, lawyer, real estate agent
and the biggest chunk of all
taken by the one who claimed
he loved me most.

This is the year I grew old
became aware of laws
careless of the lives they dislodge
designed to break down walls
to shatter this house
of strong timbers
solid as rock.

This is the year I grew old
my children and I
make our way alone,
our life ended
as sharply as the lines
I slashed on paper
reduced to a scarred
charcoal image.

Section 6

Remembrances

Idle things

I thought of phoning you today Mother–
wanting your love
wanting to be
a part of you again.

You were brave when I left
so many years ago.
Did you know,
I looked back,
saw your pain.

I wanted to run back,
to hold you near
but you would have
brushed me aside,
embarrassed,
I'd known your feelings,
known your pain.

There's so much
you've held inside.
I wanted to say,
I've cried for you–
for the part you will never
let me share.

Coast Range

When Mother visited
she said she wouldn't be able
to live in the mountains,
that they closed around her,
brought early darkness.

Unlike home, where open fields
blend into each other
and summer sun lingers,
postponing night.

When she comes again,
I hope she can bring her memory
of vast prairie, open sky,
lakes and plains.

Could she then
see beauty here?
Light glistening on ocean waves,
a line of pink turning to purple
as the sun sets,
fir trees a mantle of green
on the mountains.

His Last Year

For the first time since Mama died,
I return to visit Uncle Stanley
in the little stucco house he built
on the outskirts of Winnipeg.

It's different from the farmhouse
we all lived in years ago
with its spacious kitchen and wide veranda
overlooking fields of potatoes,
corn and scarlet runner beans
that almost overtook the railroad tracks.

This house, now a part of the city
is dwarfed by a subdivision.
There is still a field out back
though the grass is patchy stubble
and dry soil scatters in the wind.

In this, his last year of life
he talks about dying
takes me out to the cemetery
where he tends Mother's grave.

He pats the earth firmly
over seeds he has planted
and I think of him—
soon to be under that heavy earth
packed too solid to be scattered.

Thank you for completing *And Still the Sky is Pink and Blue.*

We would love if you could help by posting a review at your book retailer and on the PageMaster Publishing site. It only takes a minute and it would really help others by giving them an idea of your experience.

Thanks

PM Store Author's QR Code
https://pagemasterpublishing.ca/by/joan-hill/

www.ingramcontent.com/pod-product-compliance
Lightning Source LLC
LaVergne TN
LVHW050610100826
845148LV00015B/3206

9781773545400